What Others Are Saying

Good afternoon, Joe,

Thank you for sitting in my class each evening. I enjoyed your interaction with the other students. You gave me a copy of your book *Eternal Salvation*. Thank you. You asked my opinion; I think it is a perfect tool for witnessing and sharing your faith. It is a tool that unbelievers and Christians can use.

—Dr. Elmer L. Towns
Cofounder and Vice President, Liberty University

Dr. Towns has written over eighty books.

Hi Joe,

I was able to quickly read through your book on eternal security. It was very nice. I think it would be a good tool to use in ministry. However, I don't know what to suggest about distributing it. I am also writing a booklet on eternal security, but I will distribute that through my GraceLife network.

Maybe you can keep paper copies on hand and be willing to send a digital copy to those who might need it or use it.

I wish you all of God's success in ministry and sharing the gospel of grace. Blessings.

—Dr. Charlie Bing
GraceLife.org

Dr. Bing has written three of the best books I ever read and recommended a fourth book, Freely by His Grace. *Simply by Grace,* Free Grace Theology: 5 Ways It Magnifies the Gospel, *and* Lordship Salvation.

> I assure you and most solemnly say to you, the person
> who hears My Word and believes and trusts in Him
> who sent Me, has eternal life. (John 5:24, AMP)

As I sat to pen this foreword to this booklet, I am reminded of the cold January morning I met him in the ER at Orangeburg Regional Hospital. Joe has the zeal of the apostle Paul when he witnesses to others about eternal salvation and the assurance that it was all accomplished on the cross of Calvary.

D1714093

First, Joe wants mankind to understand that they are born sinners and they did not have anything to do with it. I think David said it well in Psalm 51:5 (NIV), "For I was born a sinner—yes, from the moment my mother conceived me."

Thirdly, Joe constantly and consistently points back to Calvary whenever he is asked to defend the content of this booklet. He honors Peter's command as in 1 Peter 3:15 (NLT) and worships Christ as Lord of his life. If someone asks about his Christian hope, he is always ready to explain it with love and respect.

While reading, you will see that Joe simply explains eight different "-tion" words (justification, redemption, reconciliation, imputation, propitiation, sanctification, salvation, and glorification) and their commonality in making it all as finished and done through the confession of sins and faith in Jesus the Christ (Rom. 10:9–11 AMP).

May God add a special blessing to the readers of this booklet.

—Rev. Dr. Belinda S. Smalls
Senior pastor at the Church House of Ministries
Worldwide, Moncks Corner, SC

This booklet is twenty-five years in the making for my dad. He is well-known throughout our community as a man who loves God, an extremely hard worker, and a man of many, many, many words. To me he is all that and more—a faithful husband and father, a giver, and someone who sees the best in everyone, just to name a few.

My dad is passionate about the message he shares in this booklet because he has studied and experienced God's grace and mercy, and he wants everyone to know not only how amazing God is but also how attainable it is. I've been blessed to have him in my life teaching my brother and me about who God is and why it is so important to have a relationship with Him. Despite living with my dad and hearing about eternal salvation for years, being a part of the editing process of this booklet has been beneficial in my spiritual journey. The most frustrating part for me is that over time, so many people have made Christianity seem like a chore when it really isn't. God loves us so much and has made it so easy to love and accept Him into our lives that is almost unbelievable. I sincerely believe that anyone who reads these words with an open heart and mind can be touched. If only one person accepts Jesus into his/her heart and becomes saved because of the information in this booklet, all the many revisions, calls, and nagging from my dad will make this experience worthwhile.

Thank you for reading.

—Jazzmine Clemons

What is Eternal Salvation?

A Big Lie or Simple Truth?

This could be the best and most important
book you have never read.
Until you know *how* and *why* eternal salvation is true,
chances are that you have not heard the truth, or true
Gospel. If you have not heard the true Gospel, the Good
News of the Gospel will never make good sense.

When you know what Salvation is, it will turn the
burden of sharing the good news of the Gospel, into a
delight and soon it could become a passion to share
The Good News of the Gospel.

This book has the best explanation of Salvation,
Christianity and what a Christian is, that I have ever read.

Joe Clemons

NEWMAN SPRINGS PUBLISHING
320 Broad Street
Red Bank, NJ 07701

First originally published by Newman Springs Publishing 2019

ISBN 978-1-64531-575-9 (Paperback)
ISBN 978-1-64531-576-6 (Digital)

Printed in the United States of America

Contents

Foreword

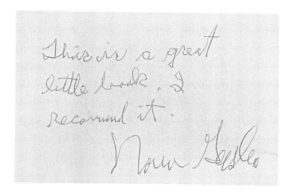

This is a great little book. I recommend it.

—Norman L. Geisler

Dr. Norman L. Geisler has written over 100 books and is considered to be a giant among giants in the field of Christian Apologetics. Some say he is the number 1 theologian in the world. He is the cofounder of the Southern Evangelical Seminary, where I am currently a student.

Personal Testimony

In 1983 at the age of twenty-three, I was your typical, average, no-good American guy. At that time in my life, as James Brown would say, "I was doing my thing." I did most of the dirty dozen, nasty nine, filthy five, and I may have done one of the slack two, but never did the unthinkable one. I got most of that from Dr. Tony Evans.

I was reared in a small community called Cross, South Carolina, where I lived with my parents and siblings, and my mom took us to church every week. After high school, I went off to technical college, where I became a welder and resided in Denmark and Columbia, South Carolina. I later moved to Tampa, Florida, for work but after a few months decided to go back home to Cross because like they say, "There's no place like home." One day in Tampa, I met a young man that was about my age (twenty-one) who had bought a house. This inspired me to build my own house (after paying rent all over the place), but although I had a new plan, I had my same old problem, not drugs, alcohol, smoking, gambling, and not even child support or alimony; I had a "she weakness"—women.

Even with my new desire to build a house, a couple of years passed, and I was still living with my mom and doing my thing. I realized that I was not making any headway with my plan, and then I remembered what Richard Pryor used to say, "Anytime you cannot stop yourself from doing what you love to do and at the very same time all the problems you got come from the things you love to do, you got a problem and need some help." At the end of every year, all I had were memories and no money, so I knew that I needed help if I was to get out of that rut.

My mom was a good Christian woman, and I saw how God was blessing and helping her. While staying with her, she always reminded me about church and the Lord. I always believed in God and that there was a heaven and hell, so I began going to church every Sunday with her. After about a month, I was convicted by the Word and Spirit and accepted Christ into my life, and the rest was history.

Well, after about two years of faithfully attending church (a Pentecostal church) and trying to be a good member and a good Christian, I began to have a problem because my church leaders told me I was saved, but that I needed to receive the Holy Ghost. At that time, I was doing everything they told me to do; I was fasting, praying, tarrying, and reading my Bible. Reading my Bible showed me that if I am saved, I have the Holy Ghost, so I started asking questions. I realized the answers I received sounded good but either were not consistent or did not make good Bible sense. Then I started to do a study on the Holy Ghost, and that's when I found out that every believer has the Holy Ghost, also that He resides or abides with us forever. This led me to see, believe, and I became convinced that eternal salvation is true. Unfortunately, sharing my understanding with my church leaders did not go well. My pastor was bishop of the state of my denomination, and he did not believe in eternal salvation. He had a son who had received a doctrine degree in theology, so I approached him in hopes that he would understand my point of view and would help convey it to his dad. After a few meetings, he expressed that he did not believe in eternal salvation, but he did believe that every Christian has the Holy Ghost. He revealed to me that he knew this was not being taught correctly, but this was the way it had been taught for years, and he did not see how anything could be done.

Experiences and conversations with church leaders through- out the years such as this fueled me to help others understand the Gospel in the right way. A few years ago, my mom and dad died as believers who did not know of the assurance we have in Christ. To this day (thirty-five years later), my siblings and most of my family, friends, community, and believers that I know don't know how good the Good News is because they do not believe in eternal salvation. For this reason, I have dedicated myself to be my family and community spiritual paralegal. This was done to give them a better understanding of the Gospel. I believe that every family needs a spiritual paralegal, one that will take the time and do the work that is needed. To help the family not get caught in dump doctrine, bad theology, cults, and false religion. My prayer is that reading this booklet will help someone begin to understand and appreciate all that God has done for us. Thank you, and I ask that you pray for me and may the Lord bless us all.

Introduction

The Gospel means Good News, and it is the best news that man will ever hear in this life, because it tells about what God has done so that we can have eternal life or to save us by his grace. Unfortunately, most people, including preachers and teachers, explain it in a way that doesn't make good sense. Most of the preachers and teachers that I know say that one must accept Christ and live right or good to be saved; however, the Bible tells us that it is impossible to live good or right enough to be saved. There is no way to see or explain the Good News about how God saved by Grace without understanding salvation, which is eternal. Those who reject God's salvation, and/or the concept of eternal salvation have incorrect knowledge of what God is offering and do not know or believe what the Gospel is truly saying. The Bible said that eternal life, and salvation, is free and a gift. Well, what does that imply? No conditions or strings attached. Remember, when what you truly know (saved by grace) doesn't match, what you really believe (live right to be saved), you have a problem and need a better understanding. Well, this book is designed to help you check on your S.I.Q., That's your spiritual intelligence and understanding. I.Q. is good for living and making a living. But your S.I.Q. is good for both, living and dying more successfully.

If you want to see people, even good Christian people who love God, become confused and even angry, ask them this question: does going to heaven depend on how you live, or does it not? I have never found a Christian who did not know that salvation is by grace. They also know that it is a gift that cannot be earned. But some of these same people will also tell you that being saved and going to heaven depends on how they live. This is a direct contradiction because that makes heaven attainable by earning it. Now I'm talking about spiritual, righteous, and committed Christians. I am talking about people who believe all the same things concerning the foundation of our faith. They will become so unspiritual, unrighteous, and angry with one another that they would almost fight. They may even stop associating or speaking with one another.

Just picture going to a big interdenominational meeting with all denominations of Christianity present and someone deciding to debate eternal salvation. Can you imagine the confusion that could or would be started just from those two words? All this confusion could be eliminated if people would just take the time to investigate. You can have a lot of knowledge about something, but until you get a good understanding of it, you just have a lot of information that you do not understand and cannot explain, that means you have a low S.I.Q.

It is amazing that all this confusion could happen to people who are united in the same belief. Even though their beliefs are the same, they could be separated by two simple words, so most people avoid this conversation. I call them the Christian's "dirty" words: **eternal salvation**—meaning that once a person is saved, he becomes a born-again believer and that he can never become unsaved. It simply means that a person is saved eternally; once saved, a person can never be lost or go to hell. I think this could be one of the oldest arguments among believers. This is the most important truth and the only and best way to understand the Gospel's message. If we could understand this concept, we would know what John 3:16 really means. We would realize what God's love has accomplished for us. If you want to see something that is unbelievable, ask your pastor or any minister, "What is salvation," and "What is the Gospel or Good News?" The Gospel is the good news that tell us what God have done so that we can be save; salvation tell us that we are saved and show us how saved we are by the presence of the Holy Spirit as a guarantee. You cannot have salvation without having the Holy Spirit.

Many of us view Christianity as a religion, but we should know that Christianity is technically not a religion—it's a new kind of **humanity** (or in other words, Christ in humanity is Christianity). But when people don't understand salvation, they turn Christianity into a religion. We must begin to see that all denominations if they are a part of Christianity, are a part of the one body of believers—the church of God's people, the body of Christ's church, all who have been reborn, all having received faith in God the same way.

I will say it again everyone who has God's salvation received it the very same way. We all received it by the preaching of God's Word or by hearing or reading the Gospel story. We heard in the Gospel how Jesus died and was raised from the dead to pay for our sins. Then through the Power of God, the Holy Spirit gave us all the ability to believe and have that faith that brings salvation.

When a person understands what it means to be saved, what it means to be saved by grace, and what it means to have salvation, he or she will not even entertain the thought that salvation can be gained or maintained depending upon how one lives. If this were true, it would totally cancel out the concept of being saved by grace alone. I can see someone being confused who does not have the truth. But please don't be confused with *the truth*.

Now if I have not offended you yet, please take the time to consider the *truth*. The only book in the world that can tell us about how God forgives and saves men is the Bible. It tells not what you believe or have been taught, but it tells the absolute truth. Let the truth correct you, direct you, encourage or discourage, build you up, or hurt your feelings. Just never let the truth offend you because if it does, you will never benefit from it.

In the next few chapters of this book, I will explain how the Bible teaches us eight different ways or aspect of how God saved us. Most of the words used are very familiar to us; however, you may not understand what all of them mean and represent, nor what they all have in common.

The words that are used are these: *justification, redemption, reconciliation, imputation, propitiation, sanctification, salvation,* and *glorification.* What do all those words have in common? They all end with the suffix *-tion,* which refers to something that has reached its goal or destination. It is in a state of completion; it is finished, accomplished, and done. Remember, *-tion* means done.

These words are more clearly explained in the New Testament. The first four books of the New Testament contain the Gospel that tells us the story about what God has done so that we can be saved.

The Gospel is the good news about God's saving grace for this human race. The Epistles, or letters, in the New Testament explain and help us to understand how this was accomplished with the power and provision of God. This is what gives us assurance about being secured eternally, or in theological terms, being assured of eternal salvation or eternal security. You can know something you have been taught, but until you under- stand what has been taught, it still does not belong to you. Eternal salvation is not just the best way—it is the *only* way to see that God saves us by grace alone. Until you believe this, you have not heard the gospel of the Bible or the true Gospel of God (Heb. 5:9). Most Christians, that love the lord and goes to church every Sunday don't believe the Truth or the Gospel. That would mean that most everyone that is not a Christian, have never even heard the Truth or True Gospel.

Grace tells us how God saves, and salvation shows us how saved we are. Anything outside of salvation by grace implies salvation by works or some human performance. If it is true that God saved by grace two thousand years ago, then it is still true today because truth cannot change. If the truth changes, it was never the truth in the beginning (Gal. 3:11, 17, 24). Remember that anything that does not come from absolute truth is absolutely a lie. Read Acts 13:38–39.

Galatians 2:21 puts it like this: "I do not frustrate (set aside) the grace of God: for if righteousness come by the law, then Christ is dead in vain." That is why I say that people who reject God's offer of salvation have confused knowledge of it, which leads to bad under- standing, and this could cause one to draw the wrong conclusion.

CHAPTER 1

Salvation and Sanctification

Salvation

Most likely, you have met or heard of people who said they were saved. Maybe you have said that they are Christians. An explanation of what they are saying is that at some point in their lives, they were born again and that they are believers and have received God's salvation.

Later, when you run into these people again, they may tell you that they are no longer saved or that they are no longer Christians. For some reason or another, they have lost their salvation and are no longer saved Christians. That mentality is common among most of our society who at one time may have attended church. This just goes to show how much people do not understand some of the things that they say.

Well, the question is this: what is salvation? Salvation can best be understood by using the word *salvaged*. All of us may have been to a salvage store or a yard salvage sale. When something is salvaged, it is kept from being destroyed and is saved for a reason. For example, if I gave you a carton containing a dozen eggs and then told you to salvage two eggs and destroy the rest, what am I telling you to do? I am telling you to destroy ten and save two. The two eggs that were salvaged are now saved and are no longer in danger of being destroyed. The two eggs have received salvation and are in a state, or position, of safety. You become the eggs' savior because you saved them.

This is what the Bible tells us: that Jesus is our Savior because He is the one who brought salvation to mankind. Titus 1:4 says, "To Titus, mine own Son after the common faith: Grace, mercy, and peace from God the Father and the Lord Jesus Christ our Savior." Also, Titus 2:11 says, "For the Grace of God that bringeth salvation hath appeared to all men." Salvation can only be attained once and only by faith or trust in what the Savior has done. Ephesians 2:8–9 says, "For by Grace are you saved through faith; and that not of yourselves; it is the gift of God: not of works, lest any man should boast." Also, in Romans 10:9–10, verse 10 says, "For with the heart man believeth unto righteousness; and with the mouth confession is made unto salvation."

Now people who reject this truth would say that this is temporary or conditional salvation. But in Hebrews 5:9, it says, "And being made perfect, He became the author (creator) of eternal salvation unto all them that obey Him." Remember now that this "obey" is not talking about work, performance, or even the Ten Commandments (that's religion). Acts 13:38 and 39 says, "Be it known unto you therefore, men and brethren, that through this man is preached unto you the forgiveness of sins: And by him all that believe are justified from all things, from which ye could not be justified by the law of Moses." If it were talking about these things, that would make them a condition for the previous verse. As I told you before, it is by faith, and it is a gift. You should know that faith has a purpose and a goal. The purpose is to get people to believe God to the point that they trust what He had said. Remember, the goal of faith is to get us to obey that which we trust, which is to attain God's salvation by becoming born of the Spirit. The Scriptures go on to say that this salvation is not only eternal, but it is also guaranteed by Jesus and the Holy Spirit. Ephesians 1:13–14 says, "In whom you also trusted, after that you heard the Word of Truth, the Gospel of your salvation: in whom also after that you believed, you were sealed with that Holy Spirit of Promise, which is the earnest (guarantee-NKJ) of our inheritance until the redemption of the purchased possession unto the praise of His glory." See also John 14:16, Ephesians 4:30, 2 Corinthians 1:22 and 5:5, and Hebrews 7:22 (NASV).

Jesus even told His disciples to wait for the comforter, which would abide (stay) with you forever (John 14:16). The problem is that people who know these scriptures do not understand it clearly the way the Bible intends. Instead, they seem to think that people will take advantage of God and His goodness, like God needs their help. What dog do they have in that fight? Well, if we let the bible do the teachings and not your parents, friends, or your favorite preacher, the only criteria to get eternal life is your faith in what the savior has done. It will get you to the grace of God that will bring salvation, instantly and eternally.

Stop and ask most Christians who say they are saved, "Tell me, what do you mean when you say you are saved?" or "What are you saved from?" They will most likely say that they are saved from sin or hell. Ask them, "Do you mean that you cannot sin or go to hell and that you are sinless? If you are saved from it, how can you still sin?" This kind of question will upset a lot of people who have knowledge, but do not have the right understanding of their salvation.

Here is another good question to ask your pastor or any minister: "What is a Christian?" They most likely will say that a Christian is one who acts like Christ or is Christlike. This is only a description of how one acts or shows what kind of Christian one is. Note that a Christian is one that has Christ in him, and that makes him a new creature that God has made (2 Cor. 5:17). He is a sinful man that has the permanent indwelling of the Holy Spirit. This is God's new creation or creature; simply put, divinity dwelling in a sinful humanity is Christianity (Rom. 8:9), and when God put the Holy Spirit in an unholy man, that's what helps an unholy man to begin to change and be more Christlike. Christ in a man is a Christian and Christ in humanity is Christianity, Christianity is not a religion, it's a new kind of humanity.

We need to understand that God basically has two major calls to mankind in this Christian era. The first and most important call is to salvation, which is eternal life; that is a call to become a Christian. The second call is to become a servant or follower of Christ; that is a call to become a disciple. There are good and bad Christians and good and bad disciples. A good Christian doesn't do bad things, and a bad Christian does. For example, Ananias and Sapphira, lying to the Holy Spirit (Acts 5:1–10), dealing with a case of incest (1 Cor. 5:1–5).

Now a disciple is one that has made the decision to obey and follow the Lord by becoming a learner, discipline, and diligent in

service to the Lord. Sometimes even the best of them failed at times, look at Peter, John Mark, and Dimas (John 18:13–27; Acts 15:38; 2 Tim. 4:10). They all have salvation and are eternally saved.

Please let me explain. Salvation in this context is referring to sin's penalty, or eternal separation from God. This context does not refer to sin's power or presence in your life. Man's total salvation has not come yet. When one dies physically, then, and only then will he be saved from sin's power, presence, or consequences. We can be or are being saved from sin's power, and one day, we will be saved from sin's presence when death comes. So now we have salvation from hell and God's wrath because we have been salvaged from going there by Jesus Christ, our Savior. Remember that a Christian is what we are, and how that Christian lives just shows what kind of Christian he is.

In 2018, I found out that some people were trying to add conditions to eternal salvation; this type of teaching is known as Lordship salvation. This teaching is incorrect because salvation is unconditional. To make it clear that salvation is unconditional and free, free grace theology explains that our salvation is eternal, free, and a gift. Jesus Christ wants to be your savior and Lord, the only requirement for eternal life is Jesus being your Savior, not Lord and Savior.

Sanctification

Have you ever heard someone describe another person to you by telling you all the things that are right and good about that person? Then on the end of the description of that person, they call him "a saint." Well, that is the world's definition of a saint. It seems like the church has adopted the world's definition of a saint rather than the Bible's definition.

The word *saint* comes from the word *sanctified ones*. The word *sanctified* means "something or someone that has been set apart." When something or someone is set apart, it is holy, and when it is holy, it is sinless. When someone is sinless, he is just as good or righteous as God, according to the Bible. In 1 Corinthians 1:2, it says, "Unto the church of God, which is at Corinth, to them that are sanctified in Christ Jesus, called to be saints, with all that in every place call upon the name of Jesus Christ our Lord, both theirs and ours."

Now the things I have just said may sound somewhat like an argument, but that is exactly what the Bible calls everyone who has

trusted Christ as their Savior. The Bible calls us saints, holy brethren, the righteous, and children and sons of God (Heb. 2:10–11). Because we have been sanctified, we have attained sanctification by God's gift of grace. In 2 Thessalonians 2:13–14, it says, "But we are bound to give thanks always to God for you, brethren beloved of the Lord, because God hath from the beginning chosen you to salvation through sanctification of (or by) the Spirit (God) and belief of the truth." See also 1 Peter 1:2. Sanctification is obtain instantaneously and permanently, because it is a spiritual position that we are in having a divine nature and we cannot even sin according to I John 3:9.

Sanctification is just one of the ways God chooses to explain how He gave us salvation. Salvation and sanctification have a lot in common. Both work in stages, or parts or tenses, to set us free from sin's penalty, power, and presence: (1) we are sanctified or have sanctification because God has set us apart from even the threat of hell (the penalty), (2) we are now called to sanctify our- selves apart from the sinful things in this world (the power), and
(3) then one day, when Jesus comes back, or when we die, we will be sanctified from the very presence of sin. Again, this will be total sanctification.

Eternal salvation is based on God, not man's ability to sanctify himself. God knows this is impossible for man to accomplish (how can an unholy, unrighteous, sinful man, keep a holy, righteous, perfect, and sinless law), which is why He sent a savior, and it is by grace, which is a gift, not by man's work. Romans 11:6 says, "If by grace, then is it no more works. But if it is of works, then is it no more Grace: otherwise, work is no more work." Also, Hebrews 10:14–15 says, "For by one offering, He (God) hath perfected forever them that are sanctified. Where of the Holy Ghost also is a witness to us: for after that He had said before."

There are a few scriptures (Col. 1:23; Eph. 5:5; Gal. 5:21) that may seem like you got to work to get saved or stay saved, but if you look and study very closely, putting them in context, you will find that this is not true. We all believe that God saved by grace, and the Scriptures cannot contradict themselves (Eph. 2:8). Everything outside of salvation or sanctification by grace alone implies work. If you believe that work plays a part, you have not yet heard the truth of the Gospel. I'm not questioning your salvation, but I am questioning your understanding of the grounds on which you have received it. Therefore, if the Scriptures can be trusted, then it's clear that being a saint does not depend on how you live—just as you know being a sinner does not depend on how one lives. Remember that more important than what you know, is how much you understand about what you know. I hope that you now understand what a true saint is. If you are not sure that you are one, pray and ask God to send Jesus into your heart and you will be sanctified and have God's sanctification forever.

CHAPTER 2

Justification and Redemption

Justification

Justification is one of those big words that has a simple meaning. It means not guilty, declared right, or free from all charges. Justification is another way that the Bible shows us how God saved man. God has promised man (Adam) that the day he ate of the tree of knowledge of good and evil that he would surely die (Gen. 2:17).

It's clear that if God had kept His promise, all of mankind would forever be lost, and if He did not, He would be unjust, unholy, and could not be a righteous God. The Almighty and Holy Creator was caught in a catch-22, so He had to come up with a way to keep His promise of punishment and save man at the same time.

Justification tells the story of how God kept his promise. Romans 3:21–28 explains how God did both: kept his word and saved sinners. Verse 26 says, "To declare, I say, at this time His (God's) righteousness: that He (God) might be just and justifier of him which believeth in Jesus." That is why no one goes to heaven or Hell because of the way one lives. The criteria is to believe what Jesus has done.

God did not forgive our sins, but He paid for them Himself. A person can only be justified before God by believing this truth. When you are justified, you have justification the very moment you believe. Romans 3:22–23 says, "Even the righteousness of God which is by faith in Jesus Christ unto all and upon all them that believe, for there is no difference: For all have sinned and come short of the glory of

God." Only faith, in what God has done, brings God's salvation and justification. Romans 4:16 says, "Therefore it is of faith, that it might be (is) by grace; to the end the promise might be sure to all the seed; not to that only which is of (keep) the law; but to that also which is of the faith of Abraham; who is the father of us all."

Those who reject eternal salvation say that this justification or righteousness that God gives us only puts us in a justified position and is not an eternal justification. But that is man telling God how things are in his sight, not God telling man according to the Bible. The Bible goes on to say that everyone whom God has justified will reach his destination of glorification.

Now if the Bible cannot contradict itself and God always keeps His promises, then these verses can be trusted. Romans 8:30–31 says, "Moreover whom He (God) did predestinate, them He also called: and whom He called, them He also justified, them He also glorified. What shall we then say to these things? If God be for us, who can be against us?" See also verses 38 and 39.

These verses are telling us what God has already considered as done, since we cannot and will not be glorified until we die. Still, God goes on to say that we are members of heaven. Philippians 3:20 says, "For our conversation (citizenship) is in Heaven; from whence (which) also we look for the Savior, the Lord Jesus Christ." Also, Romans 5:9 says, "Much more then, being justified by His blood, we shall be saved from wrath (and hell) through Him."

I am sorry if what you think and believe does not match up with what the Bible teaches. I could have used a lot more scriptures, and since the scriptures were given by God, they should make it very clear that the only way to be justified is through God's special grace, which assures us of eternal life.

That is why I am totally convinced that eternal salvation is based on God's trustworthy word. Romans 5:1–2 says, "Therefore being justified by faith, we have peace with God through our Lord Jesus Christ. By whom also we have access by faith into his grace wherein we stand and rejoice in hope of the glory of God."

There are people all over the world who have a "hope so hope." But those of us who understand and accept God's way of saving people have a "know so hope." In 1 John 5:9–13, verse 13 says, "These things have I written unto you that believe on the name of the Son of God; that you may know that ye have eternal life, and that ye may believe on the name of the Son of God." Remember that eternal life can never end—if it is eternal life, just receive Jesus into your life and you will have God's justification forever.

Redemption

Have you ever had something you loved stolen, lost, or given away that you wanted back? You later found the person who took your treasured belongings away and were told that your items were sold to a pawn shop. To get your items back, you would have to redeem them or buy back your very own items.

Well, this is the very same concept the Bible conveys about redemption, which is the theme of the entire Bible story. It tells how God, after Adam and Eve had sinned, told them and throughout the Old Testament about the promise of a Redeemer for the very purpose of man's redemption.

The redemption story reveals two things. One, it tells what God had to do to save or redeem man. Two, it shows how holy and just God is by not just putting man back in his original position instead of redeeming man. Just think, why would God, who created all things and is the rightful owner of all things, had to buy back or redeem that which He rightfully owns? Because God is holy and just. Even to the devil, He would not use His creator's right. Instead, He used his creator's wisdom to outsmart the devil and mankind. Let me explain what happened: when God created Adam, He gave Adam the authority of being the owner, overseer, and king of the earth for Him (humanly speaking).

Adam had the deed and title of the earth (so to speak). Adam was considered the god of this world (Gen. 1:28–30). But when Satan convinced Adam to disobey God's command, the devil then became the god of this world. In 2 Corinthians 4:4, it states this, and even when the devil was tempting Jesus, he told Jesus, "All these things I will give you." Jesus never told him that he did not own it (Matt. 4:8–11).

God then had to outsmart and defeat Satan's plans of taking all of mankind to hell with him. You see, hell was created for the devil and his angels. When the devil convinced Adam to sin, he knew that mankind would be condemned to hell also. Do you know that no one goes to Hell or Heaven because how they live? People go to Hell or Heaven because of one criteria, and that is "do you believe and receive that Jesus died for your sins?" Or do you not believe the gospel which tells you that Jesus died on the cross to pay for all your sins? But our all-wise God, in all His wisdom and love, freed man from this terrible end.

When God allowed Satan and the Jewish leaders by the Romans to crucify Jesus, it defeated Satan and freed us that we could be redeemed. Satan was the one who inspired the Jewish leader, Judas, to betray Jesus and have him killed. If Satan knew that this crucifixion would defeat his plans, the Bible says that he would not have done it. In 1 Corinthians 2:8, it says, "Which none of the princes of this world knew: for had they known it, they would not have crucified the Lord of Glory."

All this shows us how the all-wise God had to use His wisdom to redeem us. In 1 Corinthians 1:30 says, "But of Him (God) are you in Christ Jesus, who of God is made unto us wisdom, and righteousness, and sanctification, and redemption." This redemption is a total work of God and an eternal work of God. Ephesians 1:6–7 says, "To the praise of the glory of His grace, wherein He hath made us accepted in the beloved. In whom we have redemption through His blood; the forgiveness of sins, according to the riches of His grace."

In Hebrews 9:12, it states, "Neither by blood of goats and calves but by His own blood. He entered in once into the Holy place, having obtained eternal redemption for us." If you do not want to believe the Bible, that is your right, but please do not say that the Bible does not teach about being eternally redeemed.

Yet another example of our redemption is seen by the fact that mankind was cursed by sin when Adam sinned. God did not forgive or reverse this curse; instead, He redeemed us from it. Galatians 3:13 tells us, "Christ hath redeemed us from the curse of the law, being made a curse for us: for it is written, cursed is everyone that hangeth on a tree."

The curse was that man could not, now a sinner, obey God's law. God knows that an unholy man cannot keep a holy law, and we

were powerless to sin's power over us, so Christ freed us from that bondage Galatians 3:14 says, "That the blessing of Abraham might come on the Gentiles through Jesus Christ; that we might receive the promise of the Spirit through faith."

The Spirit of God tells us we are freed, sealed sons of God, and this guarantees us of heaven. Ephesians 1:13–14 says, "In whom you also trusted, after that you heard the Word of Truth, the Gospel of your Salvation: in whom, also, after that you believed, you were sealed with that Holy Spirit of promise, which is the Earnest (guaran- tee) of our inheritance until the redemption of purchased possession (our bodies), unto the praise of His glory."

Redemption is like salvation and sanctification in that it deals with past, present, and future. We are redeemed from sin's penalty, we are in the process of being redeemed from sin's power, and one day, we shall be redeemed from sin's presence. You can only be redeemed from going to hell by God's grace. If you are eternally redeemed, you have eternal redemption and salvation because until you receive God's Salvation, you have not done anything to change your eternal destination.

CHAPTER 3

Reconciliation, Propitiation, Glorification and Imputation

Reconciliation

Reconciliation is another one of those big words that has a relatively simple meaning. This word may be very familiar to you, especially if you have ever lost a close relationship with someone. Imagine trying all you could to bring the relationship back to what it once was. In other words, you wanted to be reconciled. When people decide that they want to be reconciled, all they usually do is say a few words to express that they are sorry. When man sinned against God's command, however, there were no words that could be spoken to correct the situation. When Adam sinned, the relationship between God and man was broken, which could not be restored until after full payment of restitution was made. Most people seem to have a hard time believing that God does not simply forgive.

The forgiveness that reconciled us back to God is based on the bill being paid (God does not forgive sins). Romans 5:9–11 says, "Much more than having now been justified by this blood, we shall be saved from wrath through Him. For if when we were enemies we were reconciled to God through the death of His Son, much more having been reconciled, we shall be saved by His life. And not only that, but we also rejoice in God through whom we have now received the reconciliation."

We call Him Savior because this work that Christ has done was to reconcile us from hell. Jesus did not die to reconcile us from sickness, trouble, problems, and certainly not physical death. All those things are the result of sin and came into the world by Adam's sin. The consequences of that sin are what cursed and corrupted man. I believe that Jesus died for the sin of Adam. Because of this, man's love for evil made him think that God was his enemy. In Colossians 1:20b–21, it says, "Having made peace through the blood of His cross. And you, who once were alienated and enemies in your mind by wicked works, yet now He has reconciled."

I believe that most people do not have a problem with the fact that God has reconciled us. Rather, they seem to have a problem with the teaching that shows we are eternally reconciled, the moment we accept Jesus. Continuing with the verses in Colossians 1:22–23, for context purposes, we can begin to see how some people could draw the wrong conclusion.

Verse 22 states, "In the body of His flesh through death, to present you holy, and blameless, and irreproachable in his sight." This verse shows the ones who believed in Jesus how secure they are in the sight of God—the only judge of man. The next verse is where some people get confused by the word *if.*

Verse 23 reads, "If indeed you continue in the faith, grounded and steadfast, and are not moved away from the hope of the gospel which you heard, which was preached to every creator under Heaven, of which I, Paul, became a minister." By keeping this verse in the right context and understanding, we know that the word *if* has many meanings in the Bible. When you look up how *if* is used in this verse, in the Greek Concordance, you will find that it means "so be that."

This helps to drive home the point that Paul is making in this passage, which is that belief in the Good News (Gospel), that Jesus is the preeminent (key) to our redemption, reconciliation, and salvation. Paul is encouraging the believers to continue to grow in the understanding of that faith, which has made us eternally blameless and holy in God's sight.

Here, Paul is not teaching the believer how he should live; he does that later in Colossians 3. He is trying to help us get a better understanding of our position, considering how God sees us. Understanding this will make us settled, grounded, and steadfast in our faith. Paul wanted us to comprehend the truth because he knew that limited knowledge leads to limited understanding, which could cause us to draw wrong conclusions. Now, if you have a better understanding and see your need to be reconciled to God, just receive Jesus into your life and you will have reconciliation with God forever.

Propitiation

Propitiation is one of those words that would make most Christians scratch their heads and throw up their hands. They would probably say, "I do not have the faintest idea what that word means." The ironic part about that is that all Christians believe what it means. Propitiation tells the story of how God made provision, in that to have pity or mercy upon us.

Propitiation, in its simplest form, means "to appease or satisfy." It helps us to understand what God had to do to satisfy the demands of His Law, to save man. Propitiation is a New Testament word that goes back to an Old Testament word, *atonement.*

Atonement is the bringing together of two who have been enemies into a relationship of peace and friendship. The word *atonement* is used once in the New Testament—in Romans 5:11—but it is known as "reconciliation," which I explained earlier, concerning what God had to do to eternally secure our salvation.

The meaning of propitiation in Romans 3:25 is a positive provision for mercy and is shown in this context in verse 24. This can only mean that our account, as sinners, before a holy God is positively settled, instantaneously, and permanently.

In verse 26, it tells how God justified His own action in saving us. In other words, the propitiation by the blood of Christ vindicates or defends God's holy character as He justifies the sinner forever.

Without the propitiation, God would be saying, "Sin may be ignored." With the propitiation in the blood of Jesus Christ, God is saying, "This is what your sin cost me, and I bore it in my Son, as I justified you."

People who love the Lord but fight against eternal salvation does not have the right understanding; it is not because the Bible does not teach it, because it does. The scripture 1 John 2:1–2 puts it like this: "My little children, these things I write unto you, that you sin not. And if any man sin, we have an advocate (supporter, backer, helper) with the Father, Jesus Christ, the righteous; and He is the propitiation for our sins: and not for ours only, but also for the sins of the whole world." See also John 3:9, which states that "everyone who has been born of God does not sin, because his seed remains in him, he is not able to sin because he has been born of God." Hebrews 2:17. God has done all that is required to satisfy His own standard. You only need to believe and receive Jesus Christ and you will have God's propitiation forever.

Glorification

To my surprise, by writing this book, I found out that the word *glorification* is not in the Bible. In the Bible, we can find the words glory, glorious, glorify, glorifying, and some others all the way to glorified.

Glorification may be a theological word, but it is just as true as all the other words we use that are not found in the Bible. For example, *trinity* or *triune* are not found in the Bible, but all Christians believe in the Father, the Son, and the Holy Ghost, which make up the trinity. Even though the word *trinity* is not in the Bible, Christians believe that all three are God. Glorification is also not found in the Bible, but it is also something that we believe in. The reason that I, and anyone else who believes in glorification, is because glorification comes from the word *glorified*, and you cannot have one without the other. The two words are inseparable, just like the words *completed* and *completion*. I will be using *glorified* in the scriptural context and talking about Jesus's resurrected body after being raised from the dead. A resurrected body cannot and will not ever grow old and die; in other words, a resurrected body is one that is glorified.

The reason that we can be sure, to the point that we know that we will reach glorification, is that the Word of God cannot lie. In Romans 8:30–31 (NIV), it reads, "And those He (God) predestined,

He also called; those He called, He also Justified; those He justified he also glorified. What, then, shall we say in response to this? If God is for us, who can be against us?"

That verse makes it very clear that everyone who God justified will reach glorification. We were justified the very second, we were saved, born again, or whatever expression you would like to use. All those terms refer to those of us who have received salvation. The very second one is *born again*. Thirty-eight to forty things is applied to the permanent status of a believer (***http://www.egracebiblechurch. org/forty.htm***). That will never change, and it does not depend on his behavior, so the question is, are we saved by what we believe or how we behave?

Our glorification is so sure that the Bible goes on to say that our citizenship is already in heaven. Philippians 3:20–21 (NIV) says, "But our citizenship is in Heaven. And we eagerly await a Savior from there, the Lord Jesus Christ, who by the power that enables Him to bring everything under His control, will transform our lowly bodies so that they will be like his glorious body." The Bible also says that we are children and heirs of God. It does not teach that we will be, but that we *are* His heirs right now. The very moment that we receive the Spirit, we become His sons by adoption and grace. This gives us the right to call God "our Father." Romans 8:16–17 says, "The Spirit itself beareth witness with our spirit, that we are the children of God; and if children, then heirs; heirs of God and joint heirs with Christ; if so be that we suffer with Him, that we may be also glorified together." See also Romans 8:21. The future of all believers who have trusted Jesus for their salvation is just as sure, secure, and clear when it comes down to our eternal destination. Remember that a Christian is what you are, not how you live and what you are is a new kind of humanity, one that has the Spirit of God living within permanently and instantaneously. For that reason, you are as Paul said "A new creation or creator" Christ in a man is a Christian 2 Cor. 5:17 and Galatians 6:15 Well, what the Bible teaches us is not to glory in that which we have accomplished, but rather let all our glorying be done in that which has been accomplished for us. Now if you want to experience glorification, just accept Jesus as your Savior and you will be glorified the very second you die.

Imputation

Imputation is the best and simplest concept one needs to understand if someone wants to know what it means to be saved, what it means to be saved by grace, and what it means to have salvation. Imputation gives us three ways to know, understand, and solve the greatest human problem: sin. Sin has consequences that carry a penalty of everlasting torment. After you believe there is a God, the next most important thing to know and understand is, how to get God's salvation, which is the only thing that can change your eternal destination.

Imputation comes from the word *impute*, which means "to attribute something to a person, or reckon something to the account of another." This sometimes takes place in a judicial manner, so that the thing imputed becomes a ground of reward or punishment.

The doctrine of imputation underlies the scripture doctrines of original sin, atonement, and justification, which are frequently mentioned in the Old Testament (Lev. 7:18, 17:4; 2 Sam. 19:19; Ps. 32:2) and New Testament (Rom. 4:6–25, 5:13, 2 Cor. 5:19; James 2:23).

I have never met a man who did not know the story of Adam and Eve and of how the original sin came into the human race; this is what caused mankind to be a sinner and sinful. The Bible teaches that man was conceived in sin in our mother's wombs, which means that we were considered sinners before we ever sinned.

The *Pictorial Bible Dictionary* says, "The story of the fall, in Genesis 2 and 3, taken regarding subsequent history of humanity as recorded in the rest of the OT, implies that Adam's sin not only affected but was imputed to his posterity. This doctrine is more fully developed in the N.T., especially in Romans 5:12–21 where Paul shows that it was by Adam's sin that death and sin entered the world and was passed to all men. All men were condemned and made sinners in Adam."

I always say that Adam made us sinners, but we determine how sinful we become. Well, when the preacher says that as human beings, there is nothing we can do to be saved or miss hell; it is true. But when the preacher says that we got to live right to be saved or to maintain our salvation by doing right, he has it wrong, is confused, doesn't know what he believes, or he doesn't believe what he knows. Here is where I will go back to the *Pictorial Bible Dictionary* and let it explain how Christ's death took care of our sins. The book calls this "Imputation of the sin of man to Christ." Although this is not expressly stated in the Bible, it is implied in the passages that affirm that Christ bore our sins and died in our places. Isaiah 53 teaches that the servant of Jehovah bore our iniquity and God caused to fall on Him the iniquity of us all. Peter had this passage in mind when he wrote that Christ, "His own self bare our sins in his body upon the tree" (1 Pet. 2:24). The same thought is expressed in 2 Corinthians 5:21, where Paul says that Christ was "made to be sin on our behalf," and Galatians 3:13, where it is said that Christ became "a curse for us." This truth is basis to the doctrine of the atonement.

Based on these facts, when the Bible teaches that Christ has paid the penalty for mankind, it is true. That is why we hear people or preachers say that no one goes to hell because of their sins. You see, Christ, the second Adam, made it right again. Men no longer got to go to hell because the penalty has been paid. That is the Gospel (the Good News). People go to hell because they will not accept Christ's payment for their sins or their unbelief of it. Heaven or Hell does not depend on how you live.

Now this is how people go to heaven or miss hell; again, I will let the *Pictorial Bible Dictionary* explain "The Imputation of Christ's Righteousness to the Believer." This is the basis of Paul's doctrine of justification, a judicial act of God by which he declares righteous, on the ground of Christ's expiatory (payment) work and imputed righteousness, those who put their faith in Christ as their Savior. The New Testament stresses that justification is free and unmerited so far as the sinner is concerned (Rom. 3:24, 5:15; Gal. 5:4; Titus 3:7). The merits of Christ's suffering and obedience are imputed to the sinner, and he is henceforth looked upon as "just in God's sight."
I am so passionate about the truth that the Bible teaches because God has two number 1 main goals for man about his Gospel. That is for all men to be saved and to know how saved they are (1 Tim. 2:4) and not to be caught in the trap of forever learning and never able to come to

the knowledge of the truth (2 Tim. 3:7).

I know that some people may think that the verse is about silly women, but a lot of men are in that boat too. Paul had the same concerns as God. He wanted people to be saved by the only one true gospel and for people to keep the truth in the Gospel. In the New Testament, the only requirement for salvation to the Jews (God's chosen people) is to repent and confess the sin of unbelief and rejection, of Jesus as their Messiah and King. To the gentiles (the rest of us), the only requirement or condition for salvation and eternal life is to believe the gospel of Jesus and you will be saved.

God knows that until one knows and understands how and why he or she is saved and on what grounds they are going to heaven, they will never have the gratitude and attitude that produces the love, which causes one to obey and serve as God intended.

Remember, Satan's number 1 weapon is deception and his goal, to keep man from the truth of what God has done for them or to take them beyond the truth so that they will not know or believe it and not be able to pass it on to future generations, accurately. Remember again that imputed righteousness is the only remedy for imputed sin (Rom. 5:12). In 2 Corinthians 5:21, it says, "For he hath made Him to be sin for us, who knew no sin; that we might be made the righteousness of God in Him."

So God offers to trade his righteousness for our sin, something of immeasurable worth for something completely worthless. How grateful we should be for his kindness to us. Now that is imputed love (John 3:16). Because of God's love for us and you see your need of His love, please receive his son Jesus into your life and you will have God's imputed righteousness forever.

Closing Comments and Summary

The eight things discussed in this booklet are not all the ways the Bible uses to explain how people come into God's eternal family. The Bible also teaches us about election, adoption, predestination, regeneration, conversion, remission, etc. Those words help us to see that salvation, from start to finish, is totally a work of grace performed by God and given to us as a gift. This is Bible knowledge 101.

This is so important for the churches of God's people to understand. Understanding God's gift of salvation will allow us, the saved, to begin to change people's minds about what the Gospel of Jesus Christ really means. The Bible story tells us how mankind had no hope of avoiding hell. But the Gospel story is the Good News that the penalty has been paid by Jesus Christ. The moment that a person accepts Jesus as his or her Savior, he or she becomes born again and is saved forever from hell, and the Lake of Fire.

The Gospel that most people hear is that if you accept Jesus, you now have a chance to avoid hell if you live a good life. That is not the message that the gospel of Jesus Christ offers. All around us, there are people who have not heard the true Gospel. This is bad, and what is worse is that some people who have heard the Gospel and received salvation have not yet come to the realization of what they received when they received salvation. Since so many people who have salvation do not know that it is eternal, they cannot appreciate or grasp the value of being saved, and they cannot admire what

God's amazing grace has done. They will not be able to fully appreciate it until they understand it. That is why I think most people attend a church's worship service do not worship God the right way (in spirit and in truth). Worship and praises to God come from an understanding, an appreciation, and out of gratitude for all that God has done.

This kind of understanding will reflect in our attitude toward serving God. It will give believers a greater drive to share with the lost world what they have received. People will want to share the truth with those who believe that going to heaven or hell depends upon how one lives. They (the lost) may have heard, as well as some who have salvation, all the teaching and preaching about God's saving grace, but until they understand that it is eternal, they have not heard the true gospel. When they hear with an understanding that being saved means that you are saved forever, only then will they have heard the true gospel of God's saving grace. The reason why people do not see the Gospel crystal clear is because most preachers front load and back load the Gospel with requirements that God does not require for one to have eternal life. An example of front load is when a preacher says that to be saved, one must repent and confess all his sins to God and make up his mind to do right. Back load is when he says now that you are saved, you must obey God and live a righteous life and you can be or will be saved. That is not the Gospel and certainly not Good News. The Bible says that we were saved under an unconditional contract, but when people don't understand, they place conditions on an unconditional contract or covenant.

Again, this is some of the basic teaching that is our offense and our defense in sharing God's Word with the lost. When you understand this, you will not be intimidated by people with high position and education. Salvation is by grace through faith. They can theorize, intellectualize, philosophize, and apologize on all the teaching about God's saving grace and salvation. However, when the dust settles, after all the big words have been used, and when you draw the bottom line and it does not match the basic foundation, you will realize that *all* other teachings (other than salvation is by grace through faith alone) are just a lot of good sounding, even believable, logical lies (Eph. 2:8–9).

What is eternal salvation?

After you get the foundation correct, you will be able to understand what the Bible says about the purpose or reason for us to live a holy life. There is a difference in a Christian and a disciple; both are saved and have salvation, that is eternal. The one that decided to obey and follow the Lord in obedience becomes a disciple. Here are three reasons to follow the Lord:

1. The first and most important one is to make sure that the salvation we have becomes visible and attractive to our family, friends, and even our enemies who don't have it.
2. Sin is not your friend. Even though you have salvation, sin can still destroy our physical lives as it does people who do not know God.
3. There are promises of blessings that come with being faithful and obedient, which you can experience in this life and in the one to come or the hereafter which is called eternal blessing.

Titus 2:11–12 says, "For the grace of God that bringeth salvation hath appeared to all men, teaching us that, denying ungodliness and worldly lusts, we SHOULD live soberly, righteously, and godly in this present world" (not must).

God certainly has a purpose for us—to live a good life—but please do not get that confused with why one goes to heaven. If you will continue to read Titus from verse 2:11 to chapter 3, you will see where Paul explains (again) that we are not saved by works (verses 5–7), and then when he gets to verse 8, he says, "This is a faithful saying and these things I will that you affirm constantly, that they which have believed in God might be careful to maintain good works. These things are good and profitable unto (all) men."

Remember that bad knowledge leads to a bad understanding, which usually causes someone to draw the wrong conclusions. The theme of the Bible, from Genesis to Revelation, is God's promise of redemption. If you do not believe in eternal salvation, what you're really saying is that God is not keeping his number one or biggest promise made to mankind. Also, he did not keep his promise made in John 3:16, and that would mean that you cannot be saved by grace through faith alone. In 1 Thessalonians 5:9–10, it says, "For God hath not appointed us to wrath, but to obtain salvation by our Lord Jesus Christ, who died for us, that whether we wake or sleep, we should live together with Him."

This is the reassurance we have about our future, based on the word of a God who cannot lie. I do not have a "hope so hope," but I have a "know so hope." Romans 5:5 says, "And hope does not disappoint us, because God has poured out His love into our hearts by the Holy Spirit, whom He has given us" (NIV), which is our guarantee from God. Now the things that I have been explaining, you could say that is my theology. Yes, and it is based on and has consistency with Bible doctrine, and if I am right, that is so sad. Because that would mean that most of the people, preachers, and Bible teachers that you and I may know have it wrong. Well, if you see the problem that I see, let's work together to be the solution and not part of the problem. Remember that the apostle Paul said in the last days that there will be a great falling away from the faith, which is the apostasy, and that means the church will be backing up from the truth it once stood for. Read 2 Thessalonians 2:3, 1 Timothy 4:1 and Luke 18:8.

If you see your need for God's forgiveness, eternal life and salvation, please pray to the Father and tell Him that you believe in the sacrifice His son, Jesus, made on the cross for you and the world. Ask Him to send Jesus into your heart and life, and when He comes, you will have forever life and eternal life with God, and God guarantees this (Col. 1:27; 2 Cor. 13:5).

This booklet was originally written about twenty-five years ago, with some changes and adding Imputation. Thank you for reading. Feel free to call, text, or e-mail me with questions or comments.

Sponsored by Clemons Welding Ministry
Produced by Ross Printing—October 2018
Joe Clemons and Grandson Cairo Clemons
Cell: (843) 906-1133
E-mail: ClemonsWelding1@gmail.com
E-mail: clemonsweldingministry2020@gmail.com

For further inspiration, validation, and education, below are the Doctrine of the Forty Things.

DOCTRINE OF THE FORTY THINGS

Introduction: God has provided forty things for the believer at the moment of faith in Christ, and nearly all of them are unique to this Church Age dispensation. These are grace gifts from God to us at the moment we trust in Jesus Christ for our salvation.

- We receive these forty things at the very moment of salvation before we have had a chance to do anything! Therefore, we obviously receive these things by grace; we don't earn or deserve them.
- All of the things are permanent except one.
- Every believer in the Church Age receives these at the moment of salvation.
- Emotions have nothing to do with the receiving of them because they are not felt.
- They are accomplished in total by God. He gives, we receive.
- The great majority of believers are not aware of these things because they have never grown spiritually from learning Bible doctrine.

1. Reconciliation:

1) Every person is alienated from God at birth, *(Rom. 3:23)*. Therefore every person needs to be reconciled to Him. It is impossible for anyone to accomplish this himself. Reconciliation is the work of Jesus Christ on the cross, which is what removed the barrier between God and man.

2) Therefore, with the barrier gone, our simple faith in Jesus Christ causes us to step over the line into eternal salvation. We are reconciled to God at the moment we believe in Christ. Reconciliation is not a process or program.

3) *2 Cor. 5:19—Namely that God, by means of Christ, reconciled the world to Himself by not imputing their sins to them.*

4) *Rom. 5:10*—*For if, while we were enemies* (in spiritual death), *we were reconciled to God by the death of His Son, much more now being reconciled, we shall be delivered by His life.*

5) *Col. 1:20*—*...and through Him* (Jesus Christ), *to reconcile all things to Himself, having made peace through the blood of the cross.*

6) Reconciliation is realized at the moment of faith in Christ. *Col. 1:22*—*Yet He has now reconciled you in the body of His flesh through death* (substitutionary spiritual death), *in order to present you before Him holy, blameless, and beyond reproach.*

2. Regeneration:

1) At the moment of physical birth, we receive the imputation of human life to our soul. But at the moment we believe in Jesus Christ, God the Holy Spirit creates a human spirit to which God the Father imputes eternal life. Just as we have soul life forever, we have eternal life forever.

2) Regeneration is the ministry of God the Holy Spirit at the moment of salvation whereby He creates a human spirit for the purpose of the imputation of eternal life.

3) This is what it means to be "born again." It is not a physical birth like Nicodemus thought (Jn. 3). It is a spiritual birth accomplished by God the Holy Spirit. We did not earn it, deserve it, or do anything for it.

4) Once we receive a human spirit, we become trichotomous, meaning that we have a body, a soul, and the newly acquired human spirit for fellowship with God.

5) We cannot understand spiritual phenomenon until we become trichotomous because spiritual things are nonsense to spiritually dead people, *I Cor. 2:10-16.*

3. Redemption:

1) Redemption views salvation from the standpoint of our being born into a slave market of sin. Jesus Christ paid for our freedom by His substitutionary spiritual death on the cross.

2) Therefore, redemption means that at the moment of our salvation, we are freed from the slave market of sin. We have now been liberated from slavery of Satan and our old sin natures.

3) While reconciliation is directed toward man and propitiation is directed toward God, unlimited atonement and redemption are directed toward sin.

4) This is documented in *__Gal. 3:13; Eph. 1:7; Tit.2:14; 1 Pet. 1:18-19__*.

4. Efficacious Grace:

1) The omnipotence of God the Holy Spirit makes the Gospel perspicuous in "common grace." Then we receive the convicting ministry of the Holy Spirit, God the Father's divine invitation to believe in Jesus Christ. When we believe in Jesus Christ, the ministry of God the Holy Spirit makes our faith effective for salvation.

2) Eph. 1:13—In whom also, when you heard the message of truth, the Gospel of your salvation (common grace); in whom also, when you believed ("efficacious grace"), you were sealed by means of the Holy Spirit.

3) So the first thing given to you at the moment of salvation was the fact that the Holy Spirit made your faith in Jesus Christ valid.

4) Efficacious grace removes any potential for someone to legitimately claim that their faith is meritorious—that they deserve some of the credit for their own salvation.

5. Eternal Life:

1) If we are going to live with God forever, we must have the life of God, which is eternal life. At the moment of faith in Jesus

Christ, God the Father imputes eternal life to our newly acquired human spirits.

2) This is documented in Jn. 3:15-16, 3:36, 10:28, 6:47; 1 Jn. 5:11-13.

3) Eternal life is imputed to us forever. We don't earn or deserve it. The unbeliever has soul life, which is everlasting life, living in the lake of fire forever. But spirit life is eternal. Eternal life is living in the presence of God forever. If eternal life could be lost, it would not be eternal.

6. Imputed Righteousness:

1) If we are going to live with God forever, we must be as good as God; therefore we must have the righteousness of God.

2) This is documented in Rom. 3:22; 1 Cor. 1:30; 2 Cor. 5:21; Phil. 3:9.

3) Rom. 3:22—...even the righteousness of God through faith in Jesus Christ for all those who believe.

4) 2 Cor. 5:21—He who knew no sin was made sin for us, that we might be made the righteousness of God in Him.

5) Unbelievers either don't know about imputed +R that comes through faith or else they don't believe it.

7. Justification:

1) With the righteousness of God imputed, we are justified, _**Rom. 3:28, 4:1-5, 25, 5:1-2, 9, 8:30; Gal.2:16, Tit.3:7**_.

2) Gal. 2:16—Nevertheless, knowing that a man is not justified by the works of the law, but through faith in Christ Jesus, even we have believed in Christ Jesus that we may be justified by faith in Christ and not by the works of the law; for by the works of the law no person will be justified.

3) Rom. 3:28—For we maintain that a person is justified by faith apart from the works of the law.

4) Tit.3:7—That being justified by His grace, we might be made heirs on the **basis of the confidence of eternal life.**

8. Positional Sanctification:

1) There are three categories of sanctification in the Christian way of life.
   a) Positional sanctification is union with the person of Jesus Christ at the moment of salvation. Every believer is <u>sanctified positionally</u> at the moment of salvation.
   b) Experiential sanctification refers to the spiritual life after salvation.
      1. Every believer is <u>experientially</u> <u>sanctified</u> when he is filled with the Holy Spirit.
      2. There is another type of experiential sanctification that is a potential and is only for believers who have reached spiritual maturity—The Winners!
   c) <u>Ultimate sanctification</u> refers to the time we receive our resurrection bodies at the Rapture.
      1. Every believer will be ultimately sanctified when he receives his resurrection body.
      2. Only mature believers will receive rewards, decorations, crowns, greater privileges, etc.
2) Positional sanctification puts every believer in union with Christ, positionally higher than angels, ***Heb. 1-2***.
3) Positional sanctification removes any basis for racial prejudice, cultural differences, social distinctions, personal antagonisms, economic barriers, ideological differences, sexual discrimination, or pre-salvation religious prejudice.

9. All Judgment Removed

1) At the moment of your salvation, all judgment is removed. You are never again subject to the Last Judgment or the lake of fire due to one simple act of faith in Jesus Christ.
2) Jn. 3:18—He who believes on Him is not judged, but he who does not believe is judged already because he has not believed in the unique person of Jesus Christ.

2) Rom 8:1—*There is, therefore, now no judgment to those who are in Christ Jesus. Heb 9:27.*

10. We are delivered from the power of the old sin nature.

1) This concept is found in ***Rom. 2:29; Phil. 3:3; Col. 2:11; Eph. 4:22ff.***

2) At the very moment we believe in Christ, we are delivered from the power and the authority of the old sin nature.

3) As soon as we choose to sin, we get back under the authority of the old sin nature. But the rebound technique is the means by which we can escape from being under the authority of the old sin nature.

11. All scar tissue is removed from the soul.

1) During our lifetime as unbelievers, we accumulate "scar tissue of the soul."

2) This scar tissue is a total hindrance to any form of permanent happiness, peace, or blessing of any kind. Therefore, that scar tissue must be removed before we can receive divine blessing.

3) At the moment we believe in Christ, scar tissue is removed, ***Isa. 43:25, 44:22.***

4) A negative, indifferent attitude towards God's Word can cause the believer to once again accumulate scar tissue on the soul.

12. The Baptism of the Holy Spirit.

1) At the moment of personal faith in Jesus Christ, God the Holy Spirit takes every new believer and enters him into union with Christ.

2) We are in union with Christ forever and ever and will never lose this relationship.

3) ***1 Cor. 12:13—By means of one Spirit, we were all baptized into one body, whether Jews or Greeks*** (Gentiles), ***slaves or free, and we were all made to drink into one Spirit.***

4) *Gal. 3:26-28*—*You are the sons of God through faith in Christ Jesus. For __all__ of you were baptized into Christ and have clothed yourself with Christ. There is neither Jew nor Gentile* (no racial distinctions in Christ)*; there is neither slave nor free* (no social distinctions in Christ)*; there is neither male nor female* (no sexual discrimination)*, and we are __all__ one in Christ.*

13. We are related to God the Son by Biblical analogy.

At the moment of salvation through faith in Jesus Christ, the Church Age believer becomes related to God the Son through eight special Biblical analogies.

1) The Last Adam and the new creation.
2) The Head and the body. As body of Christ, we are in union with the Head, the Lord Jesus Christ.
3) The Great Shepherd and the sheep.
4) The True Vine and the branches.
5) The Chief Cornerstone and the stones of the building.
6) The Great High Priest and members of the royal priesthood.
7) The Groom and the bride. Our wedding occurs after the Judgment Seat of Christ.
8) The King of Kings and the royal family of God.

14. Created a New Spiritual Species.

1) We are created a new spiritual species.
2) There are two new species in human history.
   a) The Jewish racial species began when Abraham was circumcised at age 99.
   b) The Church Age believer, at the moment of faith in Christ, becomes a new spiritual species. This is never true in any other dispensation.
3) *2 Cor. 5:17*—*Therefore, if anyone is in Christ, he is a new spiritual species. The old things have lost their power; behold, new things have come* (unique factors of the Church Age).

4)   *Gal. 6:15—For neither is circumcision anything, nor uncir- cumcision; but a new spiritual species.*

15. We are on a secure foundation.

1)   We are instantly on a secure foundation at the moment of our salvation, *1 Cor. 3:11, 10:4; Eph.2:20*.
2)   We can never be removed from or lose this secure foundation.

16. Recipients of Eternal Security.

1)   The moment we believe in Jesus Christ, we have eternal security.
2)   There are many approaches to teaching eternal security:
   a)   The logical approach, Rom. 8:32—If God (the Father) spared not His own Son on the cross, but delivered Him over to judgment, how shall He not with Him freely give us all things? All things include a security that neither we nor God can break.
   b)   The positional approach says that once we are in union with Christ, we can't break that union.
   c)   The experiential approach is found in 2 Tim.2:13— Though we deny Him, He cannot deny us.
   d)   The family approach is taught in Gal. 3:26—We are children of God through faith in Christ Jesus. At the point of our salvation, we are born into the family of God; we cannot be unborn from God's family. Once a son, always a son. Each of us will always be a child of God.
   e)   The inheritance approach is found in 1 Pet. 1:5.
   f) There is also the body of Christ approach.
3)   There is nothing God the Father, Son, or Holy Spirit can do to cancel our salvation after we believe in Jesus Christ, and there is nothing we can do either. There is no renunciation, no system of sin, no evil, no failure or blasphemy on our part that can ever cancel out our salvation.

17. Guaranteed a Resurrection Body Forever.

1) At the moment anyone believes in Jesus Christ, he is guaranteed a resurrection body, a perfect body forever.

2) *Jn. 11:25—Jesus said to her* (Martha)*, 'I am the resurrection and the life. He who believes in Me will live, even if he dies.'*

3) Dying does not keep us from having a resurrection body; only unbelief in Christ does that.

18. Entered into the Royal Family of God Forever.

1) There has never been a royal family of God before the Church Age.

2) Our Lord has three titles or patents.

   a) Our Lord's first royal title acknowledges His divine royalty as God, John 1:18, 6:46; 1 Tim 6:16; 1 Jn 4:12; Rom 1:4. These passages indicate He is the revealed member of the Godhead. His divine royal family is God the Father and God the Holy Spirit. This royal title is Son of God, Rom 1:3.

   b) Our Lord's second royal title refers to His Jewish title, which began at his birth. This title is Son of David, and the royal family is the dynasty of David.

   c) Our Lord's third royal title refers to His battlefield title, His strategic victory over Satan, and his forces during the First Advent, 1 Tim 6:15, 1:17; Rev 17:14, 19:16. This royal family of God title is King of kings and Lord of lords.

3) The moment we believe in Christ, we become a royal family member of God.

4) So all Church Age believers are royalty, but very few act like it. Royalty observes a certain protocol. God has a protocol plan for us to follow, and He expects us to learn it and to live by it.

19. The Sealing Ministry of God the Holy Spirit.

1) The Holy Spirit gave us a signature guarantee at the very moment we believed in Jesus Christ.

2) The sealing ministry of the Holy Spirit is not the same as His ministry of efficacious grace. The Greek word for "sealed" means to stamp with a signet ring or private mark for security and preservation. Nothing can change it, ***Dan. 6:7-24.***

3) It is documented in ***Eph. 1:13***—*In whom also, when you heard the message of truth, the Gospel of your salvation* (common grace)*; in whom also, when you believed* (effica- cious grace)*, you were sealed by means of the Holy Spirit. Eph. 4:20; 2 Cor. 1:22*—*Who also sealed us and gave us the Spirit in our hearts as the guarantee.*

20. The Distribution of Spiritual Gifts.

1) At the moment we believe in Christ, God the Holy Spirit provides each of us with at least one spiritual gift.

2) The initial distribution of spiritual gifts in the first generation of the Church Age was made by God the Son, ***Eph. 4:7-11***.

3) Subsequently, God the Holy Spirit provides the spiritual gifts, based on His sovereign decision. Never complain about your spiritual gift; it is based on the wise decision of God the Holy Spirit.

21. The Indwelling of God the Holy Spirit.

1) We are never commanded to be indwelt by the Spirit because at the moment of salvation, the Holy Spirit instantaneously indwells the body of the Church Age believer, ***Rom 8:11; 1 Cor 3:16, 6:19-20; 2 Cor 6:16***.

2) The Holy Spirit indwells the body of every believer for a purpose: to provide divine power to offset the continued presence of the old sin nature indwelling the body after salvation.

3) The indwelling of the Holy Spirit is also a sign of royal family status which is superior to being in the family of God, as believers in past dispensations were.

22. The Indwelling of God the Father.

1) At the moment of salvation through faith in Jesus Christ, God the Father indwells every Church Age believer, *Jn. 14:23; Eph. 4:6, I John 2:23*.

2) The indwelling of God the Father is for a purpose.

   a) It is related to the glorification of His protocol plan, *Eph. 1:3, 6, 12.*

   b) It is a guarantee of His personal ministry to every believer:

23. The Indwelling of God the Son.

1) The Prophecy of the Indwelling of Jesus Christ, *Jn. 14:19-20*.

2) At the moment of salvation, God the Son indwells the body of every believer; this is unique to the Church Age, *Jn. 14:20, 17:22-23; Rom. 8:10; Gal. 2:20; Col. 1:27.*

3) The purpose of the indwelling of Jesus Christ:

   a) It is a guarantee of eternal life for every believer, *1 Jn. 5:11-13*.

   b) It is the basis for assigning #1 priority to Bible doctrine which is basic to the principle of occupation with the person of Christ.

4) The indwelling of Christ is related to the Shekinah Glory in the Old Testament.

   This term is used to express the invisible presence of God the Son with Israel.

24. The Unique Protocol Plan of God.

1) We enter this protocol plan of God (PPG) at salvation.

2) The PPG is revealed in the Word of God and is designed to teach believers how to do a right thing in a right way.

3) "Protocol" refers to a rigid, longestablished code and procedure, prescribing complete deference to superior rank and authority, followed by strict adherence to due order and precedence, coupled with precisely correct procedure.

4) It educates believers as to proper procedure, following the chain of command that God has designed for the physical and spiritual realms. We did an indepth study of the PPG, August of 1999.

25. Beneficiaries of Problem Solving Devices

1) At the moment we believe in Christ, whatever problems we have had in the past, and whatever our inadequacies, God makes available to us ten problem solving devices.

2) Like the other forty things, we are not aware of these problem solving devices at the point of our salvation. Awareness comes through post-salvation Bible study.

3) These problem solving devices are exclusive to the believer only.

   a) **#1 THE REBOUND TECHNIQUE** is the only way we can recover fellowship with God after we have sinned. We simply name our sins, and according to *I Jn.1:9*, we are forgiven. Rebound is all grace; no human works, human merit, or penance can be added. This is because in rebound, we are simply citing, naming, or acknowledging a sin already judged on the cross.

   b) #2 The filling of the HOLY Spirit results from using rebound.

   c) #3 The faith-rest drill mixing the promises of God with our faith. This is how we develop a strong faith by meeting our problems with promises we find in the Bible.

   d) #4 Grace orientations coming to the realization that we do not earn or deserve salvation any blessings from God.

   e) #5 Doctrinal orientation is the constant need to put doctrine first in our lives and to function under the perception and application of Bible doctrine.

   f)) #6 Personal love for God the Father is our motivational virtue.

   g) #7 Impersonal love for all mankind is our functional virtue, the only way in which we can handle people problems

   h) #8 +H is sharing the happiness of God.

i)   #9 A personal sense of destiny.

j)   #10 Occupation with the person of Jesus Christ.

26. Beneficiaries of Propitiation

1) While reconciliation is directed toward mankind, propitiation is directed toward God.

2) Propitiation means that God the Father is satisfied with the work of Jesus Christ on the cross. God the Father is only satisfied with one person in history, Jesus Christ, because He remained impeccable throughout the thirty-three years of his lifetime as well as when bearing our sins on the cross.

3) When we believe in Jesus Christ, we are the beneficiaries of that propitiation. God the Father is satisfied with the work of Christ on the cross, and since we believe in Christ who performed it, God the Father is satisfied with us as individuals positionally.

4) This is documented in _**Rom. 3:22-26; 1 John 2:2, 4:10**_.

5) _**Rom. 3:24-25—Being justified as a gift by His grace, through the redemption that is in Christ Jesus; whom God the Father has publicly displayed by His blood as the mercy seat through faith in Christ for a demonstration of His integrity, because of the passing over of previously committed sins, because of the clemency of God.**_

   a)   The blood was sprinkled twice on the mercy seat on the Day of atonement, once for the priest and once for the people.

   b)   The mercy seat was constructed of wood and gold. Inside were three items that spoke of the sins of Israel. On each side was a gold cherub: one represented the righteousness of God; one represented the justice of God.

   c)   When the high priest came into the Holy of Holies twice on the Day of Atonement, he sprinkled blood over the top of the Ark of the Covenant or mercy seat. That blood represented the saving work of Christ on the cross.

   d)   The righteousness of God looked down and was satisfied because Jesus Christ was perfect in His humanity. The justice of God judged those sins, and God the Father was satisfied with His own judgment.

e)   Therefore, propitiation means that God the Father is satisfied with one offering only, the efficacious offering of our Lord Jesus Christ.

27. Equal Privilege and Equal Opportunity to receive escrow blessings

1)   There is only one thing in life that makes people equal, and that is what God does for all believers at the moment they believe in Christ.

2)   At the moment of our salvation, we are given equal privilege and equal opportunity.

3)   Equal privilege is part of our royal priesthood; equal opportunity is part of logistical grace.

4)   Equal privilege is provided in positional sanctification; equal opportunity is provided in the operational-type divine dynasphere.

28. An Eternal Inheritance

1)   At the moment we believe in Christ, we receive an inheritance which is eternal. We become the heirs of God. We cannot earn or deserve this.

2)   *Eph. 1:14—Who is the guarantee of our inheritance for the release of your assets for the praise of His glory. Eph. 1:18; Rom. 8:17; Gal. 3:29, 4:6-7; Eph. 3:6; 1 Pet. 1:4, 3:7; Heb. 9:15.*

3)   *1 Pet. 1:4—We have an inheritance incorruptible, undefiled, that fades not away, reserved in heaven for those who are kept by the power of God through faith unto salvation, ready to be revealed in the last time.*

4)   *Heb. 9:15—And for this reason, He is the mediator of a new covenant, in order that since a death has taken place for the redemption of the transgressions* (committed under the first

covenant)*, those who have been called* (divine invitation) *may receive the promise of eternal inheritance.*

29. Beneficiaries of Unlimited Atonement

1) Unlimited atonement means that Jesus Christ was judged on the cross for all personal sins in the history of the human race, from the first sin of Adam to the last sin committed in the Millennium.
2) Unlimited atonement means that salvation is open to anyone who will believe in Christ. Only those who believe in Christ become the beneficiaries of unlimited atonement.
3) This is documented in *2 Cor 5:14-15, 19; 1 Tim 2:6, 4:10; Tit 2:11; Heb 2:9; 2 Pet 2:1; 1 Jn 2:2.*

30. The Universal Priesthood of the Believer

1) Only in this dispensation is every believer appointed a priest at the moment of salvation, *1 Pet 2:5,9; Rev 1:6, 5:10, 20:6*.
2) As a priest, every believer represents himself before God. Unlike the Levitical priesthood of the Mosaic Law, today, women are included in the priesthood.

31. The Royal Ambassadorship of the Believer

1) At the moment of salvation, each one of us is appointed a royal ambassador. This is unique to the Church Age.
2) 2 Cor 5:20—Therefore, we are ambassadors for Christ, as though God were making His appeal through us. We invite you, on behalf of Christ, become reconciled to God.
3) Since you are an ambassador, a part of your responsibility is witnessing for Jesus Christ. It is your responsibility to make the issue clear, for God the Holy Spirit is the sovereign executive of personal witnessing.

32. Election is Realized

Election is a technical term used for believers only, ***Eph. 1:4.***

33. Predestination is Realized

Predestination is a technical term used for believers only, ***Eph 1:5***.

34. The Unique Availability of Divine Power

1) At the moment of salvation through faith in Jesus Christ, we have three categories of divine power available—such an unprecedented extension to every believer. Available to us is:
   a) The omnipotence of God the Father is related to our portfolio of invisible assets and our eternal security, ***I Pet. 1:5. 2 Cor. 12:10 Phil. 4:13***.
   b) The omnipotence of God the Son is related to the preservation of the universe and the perpetuation of human history, Job 38:16-41.
   c) The omnipotence of God the Holy Spirit provides the enabling power for the perception of Bible doctrine which is the power base for executing the protocol plan of God, ***Matt. 22:29 I Cor. 2:5 Eph. 3:16 Col. 1:10-11.***
2) The fact that this divine power is available at salvation does not imply that most believers today ever utilize this power. In fact, most believers are powerless and useless because of ignorance of Bible doctrine.

35. Deliverance from the Kingdom of Satan

1) At the moment you believe in Christ, you are delivered from the authority of Satan. ***Col. 1:13a—For He delivered us from the authority of darkness.***
2) At the moment we believe in Christ, salvation removes us from cosmic involvement. All unbelievers are in the cosmic

system under spiritual death and the absolute control of the old sin nature.

3) For some who are demon-possessed, salvation through faith in Christ removes demon possession. For others who are demon influenced, salvation through faith in Christ removes demon influence.

36. Transferred into the Kingdom of God

1) At the moment of our salvation, we are transferred into the kingdom of God.
   Col. 1:13b—And He transferred us into the kingdom of the Son of His love.

2) Therefore, everything that happened to us before salvation that could be a handicap in our lives has been eliminated. This includes whatever we were and however we failed.

3) Therefore, the only way that anything that happened to you before salvation can be a handicap is if you make it a handicap because of ignorance of Bible doctrine and ignorance of God's policy of grace.

37. We are given access to God

The moment we believe in Christ, we start having access to God through prayer,
Rom. 5:2; Eph. 2:18; Heb. 4:14, 16,10:19-20.

38. We are a gift from God the Father to God the Son

We are a gift in that we are formed as the royal family of God, **_Jn 10:22-29, 17:2,6,9_**.

39. Escrow Blessings

1) Billions of years ago, God the Father, as the Grantor, deposited into escrow greater blessings for each of us. In His omniscience,

He knew we would believe in Christ. So He deposited into escrow greater blessings for both time and eternity.

2) These blessings are irrevocable. We Church Age believers are the grantees. At the moment we believe in Christ, these blessings become applicable or available.

3) By growing in grace after salvation to spiritual maturity, we receive our escrow blessings for time. Then at the Judgment Seat of Christ, we will receive our escrow blessings for the eternal state.

4) All Church Age believers have equal privilege and equal opportunity to advance to spiritual maturity and receive these greater blessings, *James 4:6.*

5) However, many believers are losers instead of winners in that they fail to use these opportunities. Because they are not consistent learning Bible doctrine, their escrow blessings remain on deposit in heaven forever. Since the blessings are irrevocable, they either remain on deposit for losers, or they are distributed to winners.

6) Escrow Blessings, *Super Grace Blessings*, come in six categories:
Spiritual Blessings
Temporal Blessings
Blessings by Association
Historical Impact
Undeserved Suffering
Dying Grace

SUPERGRACE BLESSINGS

1. **Spiritual blessings**.
   a. Sharing the perfect happiness of God, occupation with Christ.
   b. Capacity for life, love, happiness, blessing, and total appreciation for grace.
   c. The ability to face undeserved suffering in life.
   d. The ability to correctly interpret contemporary history, to evaluate current events in the light of the Word of God.

e. Freedom from slavery to circumstances in life and adaptability to changing circumstances. The mature believer is the greatest innovator in time of historical disaster.

f. Grace-orientation, freedom-orientation, authority-orientation, common sense.

g. A total sense of security, whether in prosperity or disaster.

2. **Temporal blessings**

   a. a. Wealth, either received as a gift or acquired.

   b. Professional prosperity: great influence, leadership dynamics, success, promotion, recognition in one's sphere of life. When God promotes you, you are qualified for the job. The ability to assume responsibility and authority.

   c. Social prosperity: great friends.

   d. Sexual prosperity with one's own husband or wife.

   e. Technical prosperity or mental prosperity: the ability to think; concentration increases.

   f. Cultural prosperity: maximum enjoyment of drama, art, literature, music, history.

   g. Establishment prosperity: enjoyment of freedom, privacy, protection of life and property from criminals and reprisal.

   h. Health.

3. **Blessings by association**

   a. Those around a mature believer are blessed by their association or relationship with that person. They are blessed either directly by God or indirectly from the supergrace believer's overflow of supergrace blessings. Others share in the blessings of the supergrace believer.

   b. There are peripheral areas of blessing by association: loved ones, business life, social life, and the local church.

   c. There are also geographical blessings shared by the supergrace believer's city, state, and nation.

4. **Historical blessing**

   The mature believer carries his generation, **2 Tim 1:5**. He stabilizes his generation and becomes a stabilizer for future historical generations. The ebb and flow of history does not disturb the tranquility or impact of the mature believer. The reversionist is caught up in the disasters of history and swept along with them. But the supergrace believer rides on the crest of the wave of blessing. He rises above historical disaster.

5. **Undeserved Suffering**

   a. Only in time does God have the opportunity to give us pressure, disaster, and undeserved suffering to prove to Satan and the fallen angels that Bible doctrine can handle any situation.

   b. Suffering never leaves the believer the same as he was before. It make him either better or worse. God gives us the ability to handle suffering and to turn suffering into blessing, Rom 8:28.

   c. No rebound or soul-searching is involved because a mature believer knows when he is under divine discipline or undeserved suffering. The former is unbearable suffering, the latter is bearable.

   d. The supergrace believer's ability to handle undeserved suffering glorifies God and becomes evidence against Satan in his appeal trial.

   e. Undeserved suffering is also used by God to help you keep your eyes on God and your focus an eternity, **Rev. 2:10; 2 Cor. 12:9-10**.

   f. Undeserved suffering teaches us the value of Bible doctrine, Ps. 119:67-71.

   g. Undeserved suffering is designed to manifest the ministry of God the Holy Spirit, 2 Cor. 4:8-11.

   h. Undeserved suffering is designed to put muscle on your faith and put the focus of believers on eternal values, **Rom.8:36, 5:3-5**.

6. **<u>Dying blessings or Dying Grace</u>**

   a. Every believer has a choice in time between being positive to Bible doctrine and receiving dying grace, or being negative to doctrine and dying the sin unto death.

   b. There is a relationship between the supergrace blessings for time and the eternal rewards and blessings at the Judgment Seat of Christ.

   c. Dying grace is the link between the two. It bridges the gap. From saving grace, we go to logistical grace, then to supergrace, through dying grace, to surpassing grace, Heb 11:13.

   d. The curse of death with its pain and fear is removed. It is the greatest experience in life. It is the antithesis of the sin unto death. The perfect happiness of the supergrace believer in time is exceeded by his +H in dying grace.

   e. Therefore, the mature believer has the best of life, better in dying, and better than the best for all eternity. Ps 116:15— Precious in the sight of the Lord is the death of His godly ones.

   f. Saving grace, attained by faith in Christ, advances us into the royal family forever.

   <u>Logistical grace</u> keeps us alive in phase two of the plan of God (time) for the attainment of blessing or discipline.

   <u>Supergrace</u> is the provision of maximum blessing for the mature believer.

   <u>Dying grace</u> is the bridge between supergrace blessings for time and surpassing grace blessings for eternity.

   <u>Surpassing grace</u> is the rewards and decorations belonging to the mature believer at the Judgment Seat of Christ.

40. The Filling of the Holy Spirit

1) This occurs for the first time at the moment of salvation through faith in Christ.

2) At the moment we believe in Christ, we are filled with the Holy Spirit. None of us retain this status for very long. How often we regain that status, or **IF** we regain it depends on the knowledge we acquire about spirituality and God's plan for our lives.

3) The only way to recover the filling of the Holy Spirit and obey the mandate given in **_Eph. 5:18_** is through the use of the rebound technique (confession of sin to God the Father).
4) The filling of the Holy Spirit is unique to this dispensation.
   a) The enduement of the Holy Spirit for some believers in the O.T. was different:
   b) It was not available to every believer, it was given to achieve a specific mission, and it was withdrawn when the mission was completed.
   c) There are two positive mandates regarding the filling of the Holy Spirit, **_Eph. 5:18, Gal. 5:16_**.
5) There are two negative mandates regarding the filling of the Holy Spirit, **_Eph. 4:30a, I Thess. 5:19_**.
6) The filling of the Holy Spirit is not related to emotions, speaking in tongues, hearing voices, seeing visions, healing the sick, or performing miracles.
7) This in no way minimizes the function or the power or work of the Holy Spirit.
   Apart from the filling of the Holy Spirit, there is no spiritual life. It is not an end in itself but the means to an end.

Conclusion:

1) The believer should be made aware of these forty things as soon as possible after salvation so that he can express his positive volition by choosing spiritual growth and glorification of God over pseudo emotional spirituality and self-aggrandizement.
2) These forty things all received at salvation are the basis for grace-orientation, experiential sanctification, execution of the protocol plan of God, and glorification of God.

Reference:

http://www.countrybiblechurch.us/40Things/Notes/40Things.doc
To find what a lot of other ministries had said about the Forty Things received at Salvation, just google to find 40 things received at Salvation.

About the Author

I became a Christian in 1983, and it was the best decision I have made for dying and for living. I have a caring, loving family—my wife of thirty-three years and two sons and a daughter. I have written three booklets: *An Open Letter to the Human Race*, *The Solutions to Life's Greatest Problems*, and this one, *What is Eternal Salvation: A Big Lie or Simple Truth*. My prayer is that God will continue to direct and bless all of us to do His will.